TRIASSIC PERIOD • TRIASSIC PERIOD • TRIASSIC PERIOD • TRIASSIC PERIOD • TRIASSIC PERIOD • TRIASSIC PERIOD • TRIASSIC PERIOD • TRIASSIC PERIOD • TRI

...LONIA AVIPES AZENDOHSAURUS BLIKANASAURUS CAMELOTIA CAMPOSAURUS

...PERIOD • TRIASSIC PERIOD • TRIASSIC PERIOD • TRIASSIC PERIOD • TRIASSIC PERIOD • TRIASSIC PERIOD • TRIASSIC PERIOD • TRIASSIC PERI

...ATOSUCHUS DOLICHOSUCHUS EFRAASIA EOCURSOR EORAPTOR EUSKELOSAURUS

• CRETACEOUS PERIOD • CRETACEOUS PERIOD • CRETACEOUS PERIOD • CRETACEOUS PERIOD • CRETACEOUS PERIOD • CRETACEOUS PERI

...SAURUS AUSTROSAURUS AVACERATOPS AVIMIMUS BACTROSAURUS BAGACERATOPS BANBIRAPTOR BARYONYX BECKLESPINAX BEIPIAOSAURUS BOROGOVIA

...IOD • CRETACEOUS PERIOD • CRETACEOUS PERIOD • CRETACEOUS PERIOD • CRETACEOUS PERIOD • CRETACEOUS PERIOD • CRETACEOUS P

...SSIC PERIOD • JURASSIC PERIOD • JURASSIC PERIOD • JURASSIC PERIOD • JURASSIC PERIOD • JURASSIC PERIOD • JURASSIC PERIOD •

...NG OF THE JURASSIC PERIOD, THE SUPER-CONTINENT PANGAEA HAD SPLIT INTO TWO LANDMASSES

...RASSIC PERIOD • JURASSIC PERIOD • JURASSIC PERIOD • JURASSIC PERIOD • JURASSIC PERIOD • JURASSIC PERIOD • JURASSIC PERIOD • JUR

...ACHIOSAURUS BRACHYTRACHELOPAN CAMARASAURUS CAMPTOSAURUS CERATOSAURUS CETIOSAURISCUS CH...YANGSAURUS CHIALINGOSAURUS

...CRAEOSAURUS DILOPHOSAURUS DIPLODOCUS DRYOSAURUS DUBREUILLOSAURUS ELA...EUHELOPUS EUROPASAURUS

...SSIC PERIOD • JURASSIC PERIOD • JURASSIC PERIOD • JURASSIC PERIOD • JURASSIC PERI...RIOD • JURASSIC PERIOD • JU

• CRETACEOUS PERIOD • CRETACEOUS PERIOD • CRETACEOUS PERIOD • CRETACEOUS PERI...EOUS PERIOD • CRETACEOUS PERIOD • CRETACEOUS PERI

...ISDUS ERKETU ERLIKOSAURUS EUOPLOCEPHALUS FUKUIRAPTOR FUKUISAURUS GALLIMIMUS GARUDIMIMUS GASPARINISAURA GASPONIA

...ARM, WITH MORE DISTINCT WEATHER SEASONS DURING THE LATE CRETACEOUS • THE CRETACEOUS SAW INTENSE AND

...ORMS • MOUNTAIN RANGES, SUCH AS THE ROCKY MOUNTAINS IN THE WESTERN USA, WERE BEGINNING TO FORM

...US HOMALOCEPHALE HYLAEOSAURUS HYPACROSAURUS HYPSELOSAURUS HYPSILOPHODON IGUANODON INDOSUCHUS INGENIA IRRITATOR

...US PERIOD • CRETACEOUS PERIOD • CRETACEOUS PERIOD • CRETACEOUS PERIOD • CRETACEOUS PERIOD • CRETACEOUS PERIOD • CRETACE

...PERIOD • TRIASSIC PERIOD • TRIASSIC PERIOD • TRIASSIC PERIOD • TRIASSIC PERIOD • TRIASSIC PERIOD • TRIASSIC PERIOD • TRIASSIC PERIO

...AURUS ISANOSAURUS KEICHOUSAURUS LESSEMSAURUS LIKHOELESAURUS

...TRIASSIC PERIOD • TRIASSIC PERIOD • TRIASSIC PERIOD • TRIASSIC PERIOD • TRIASSIC PERIOD • TRIASSIC PERIOD • TRIASSIC PERIOD • TRIAS

...IOD • JURASSIC PERIOD • JURASSIC PERIOD • JURASSIC PERIOD • JURASSIC PERIOD • JURASSIC PERIOD • JURASSIC PERIOD • JURASSIC PERIO

...HESPEROSAURUS HETERODONTOSAURUS ICHTHYOSAURUS JANENSCHIA JINGSHANOSAURUS JURAVENATOR

...GOSAURUS MAMENCHISAURUS MARSHOSAURUS MASSOSPONDYLUS MEGALOSAURUS METRIACANTHOSAURUS

...D THE EARTH TO BECOME WARM AND HUMID • MANY OF THE DESERTS OF THE TRIASSIC WERE REPLACED BY LUSH RAINFORESTS

...PERIOD • JURASSIC PERIOD • JURASSIC PERIOD • JURASSIC PERIOD • JURASSIC PERIOD • JURASSIC PERIOD • JURASSIC PERIOD • JURASSIC P

DISCARDED

...TRIASSIC PERIOD • TRIASSIC PERIOD • TRIASSIC PERIOD • TRIASSIC PERIOD • TRIASSIC PERIOD • TRIASSIC PERIOD • TRIASSIC PERIOD • TRIASS

...RIOR TO THE TRIASSIC, NEARLY ALL MARINE SPECIES AND MANY LAND CREATURES HAD DIED OUT

...C PERIOD • TRIASSIC PERIOD • TRIASSIC PERIOD • TRIASSIC PERIOD • TRIASSIC PERIOD • TRIASSIC PERIOD • TRIASSIC PERIOD • TRIASSIC PER

...RUS MELANOROSAURUS MUSSAURUS NAMBALIA NEWTONSAURUS PANTYDRACO

...D • TRIASSIC PERIOD • TRIASSIC PERIOD • TRIASSIC PERIOD • TRIASSIC PERIOD • TRIASSIC PERIOD • TRIASSIC PERIOD • TR

...ACEOUS PERIOD • CRETACEOUS PERIOD • CRETACEOUS PERIOD • CRETACEOUS PERIOD • CRETACEOUS PERIOD • CRETACEOUS PERIOD • CR

...N RANGES • CHALK IS A ROCK THAT IS CHARACTERISTIC OF THE CRETACEOUS • WITH THE INCREASE OF VOLCANIC

...Y OF INSECTS • DUE TO THE FIRST APPEARANCE OF BEES, FLOWERING PLANTS BEGAN TO SPREAD AND EVOLVE

...IOD • CRETACEOUS PERIOD • CRETACEOUS PERIOD • CRETACEOUS PERIOD • CRETACEOUS PERIOD • CRETACEOUS PERIOD • CRETACEOUS P

...RATOPS LEPTOCERATOPS LIAOXIORNIS LIGABUESAURUS LOPHORHOTHON LURDUSAURUS MAGYAROSAURUS MAIASAURA MIALUSSAURUS

...OTYRANNUS NANSHIUNGOSAURUS NEMEGTOSAURUS NEOVENATOR NEUQUENSAURUS NIGERSAURUS NIPPONOSAURUS NOASAURUS NOTOCOLA NOTHRONYCHUS

...LS PARALITITAN PARASAUROLOPHUS PAWPAWSAURUS PELICANIMIMUS PELOROSAURUS PENTACERATOPS PINACOSAURUS PLATYCERATOPS PLEUROCOELUS

...OUS PERIOD • CRETACEOUS PERIOD • CRETACEOUS PERIOD • CRETACEOUS PERIOD • CRETACEOUS PERIOD • CRETACEOUS PERIOD • CRETA

...INCLUDING MASSIVE HERBIVORES (PLANT EATERS) AND VORACIOUS CARNIVORES (MEAT EATERS), DOMINATED THE LAND

...SSIC PERIOD • JURASSIC PERIOD • JURASSIC PERIOD • JURASSIC PERIOD • JURASSIC PERIOD • JURASSIC PERIOD • JURASSIC PERIOD • JURAS

...US POEKILOPLEURON PROCERATOSAURUS RHOETOSAURUS SARCOSAURUS SAUROPHAGANAX SCELIDOSAURUS SCUTELLOSAURUS

...JURASSIC PERIOD • JURASSIC PERIOD • JURASSIC PERIOD • JURASSIC PERIOD • JURASSIC PERIOD • JURASSIC PERIOD • JURASSIC PERIOD • JU

...TRIASSIC PERIOD • TRIASSIC PERIOD • TRIASSIC PERIOD • TRIASSIC PERIOD • TRIASSIC PERIOD • TRIASSIC PERIOD • TRIASSIC PERIOD • TRIAS

...PROTOSUCHUS RIOJASAURUS RUEHLEIA SALTOPUS SATURNALIA SELLOSAURUS

...A SINGLE GIGANTIC SUPER-CONTINENT CALLED PANGAEA, WHICH WAS CENTERED NEAR THE EQUATOR

...IC PERIOD • TRIASSIC PERIOD • TRIASSIC PERIOD • TRIASSIC PERIOD • TRIASSIC PERIOD • TRIASSIC PERIOD • TRIASSIC PERIOD • TRIASSIC PER

...EOUS PERIOD • CRETACEOUS PERIOD • CRETACEOUS PERIOD • CRETACEOUS PERIOD • CRETACEOUS PERIOD • CRETACEOUS PERIOD • CRETA

...TO THE VARIOUS CLIMATES • THE CRETACEOUS ENDED WITH A MASS EXTINCTION, AND SCIENTISTS DON'T

...RACHISAURUS RUGOS...SAICHANIA SALTASAURUS SAUROLOPHUS SAUROPELTA SAURORNITHOIDES SECERNOSAURUS SHAMOSAURUS SHANTUNGOSAURUS

...S STRUTHIOSAURUS STYGIMOLOCH STYRACOSAURUS SUCHOMIMUS SUPERSAURUS TALARURUS TANIUS TARBOSAURUS TARCHIA TELMATOSAURUS

...RE DINOSAURS TO DIE FROM STARVATION • EVENTUALLY THE CARNIVORES PERISHED FROM THE LACK OF PREY

...AGIA URBACODON UTAHRAPTOR VALDOSAURUS VELOCIRAPTOR WANNANOSAURUS WUERHOSAURUS ZALMOXES ZEPHYROSAURUS ZUNICERATOPS

...ACEOUS PERIOD • CRETACEOUS PERIOD • CRETACEOUS PERIOD • CRETACEOUS PERIOD • CRETACEOUS PERIOD • CRETACEOUS PERIOD • CR

...D • TRIASSIC PERIOD • TRIASSIC PERIOD • TRIASSIC PERIOD • TRIASSIC PERIOD • TRIASSIC PERIOD • TRIASSIC PERIOD • TRIASSIC PERIOD • TR

...S TEYUWASU THECODONTOSAURUS THOTOBOLOSAURUS VELOCIPES ZUPAYSAURUS

...WERE NO DINOSAURS • TURTLES, FROGS, LIZARDS, AND SNAKES BEGAN TO APPEAR DURING THIS TIME

...IC PERIOD • TRIASSIC PERIOD • TRIASSIC PERIOD • TRIASSIC PERIOD • TRIASSIC PERIOD • TRIASSIC PERIOD • TRIASSIC PERIOD • TRIASSIC PER

...JURASSIC PERIOD • JURASSIC PERIOD • JURASSIC PERIOD • JURASSIC PERIOD • JURASSIC PERIOD • JURASSIC PERIOD • JURASSIC PERIOD • JU

...ON YANDUSAURUS YANGCHUANOSAURUS YIMENOSAURUS YINGSHANOSAURUS YUANMOUSAURUS YUNNANOSAURUS

...HE OCEANS • BIRDS MADE THEIR FIRST APPEARANCE DURING THE JURASSIC • THE PTEROSAURS RULED THE SKIES

...D PERIOD • JURASSIC PERIOD • JURASSIC PERIOD • JURASSIC PERIOD • JURASSIC PERIOD • JURASSIC PERIOD • JURASSIC PERIOD • JURASSIC

alphaSaurs and other prehistoric types

ion dedication dedication dedication dedication dedication dedication dedication

TO STERLINGOSAURUS AND ERNESTODON, OUR LITTLEST DINOS.

nks thanks thanks thanks thanks thanks thanks

A SPECIAL THANKS TO OUR NON-EXTINCT INTERN, CARLY WRIGHT, FOR HER DEDICATION TO THE LETTER-BY-LETTER
RECONSTRUCTION OF MANY OF THE ALPHASAURS AND THE EXCAVATION OF FACTS.

INTRODUCTION KINDLY WRITTEN BY OUR FRIEND, JOE WEISMANN. THANKS, JOE!

thanks to Michael Berglund, paleo-artist & dino-digger, for his careful review of the text and art.

publisher publisher publisher publisher publisher publisher

Published in the United States 2012 by Blue Apple Books 515 Valley Street, Maplewood, NJ 07040

www.blueapplebooks.com

09/12 First Edition ISBN: 978-1-60905-193-8
PRINTED IN CHINA 1 3 5 7 9 10 8 6 4 2

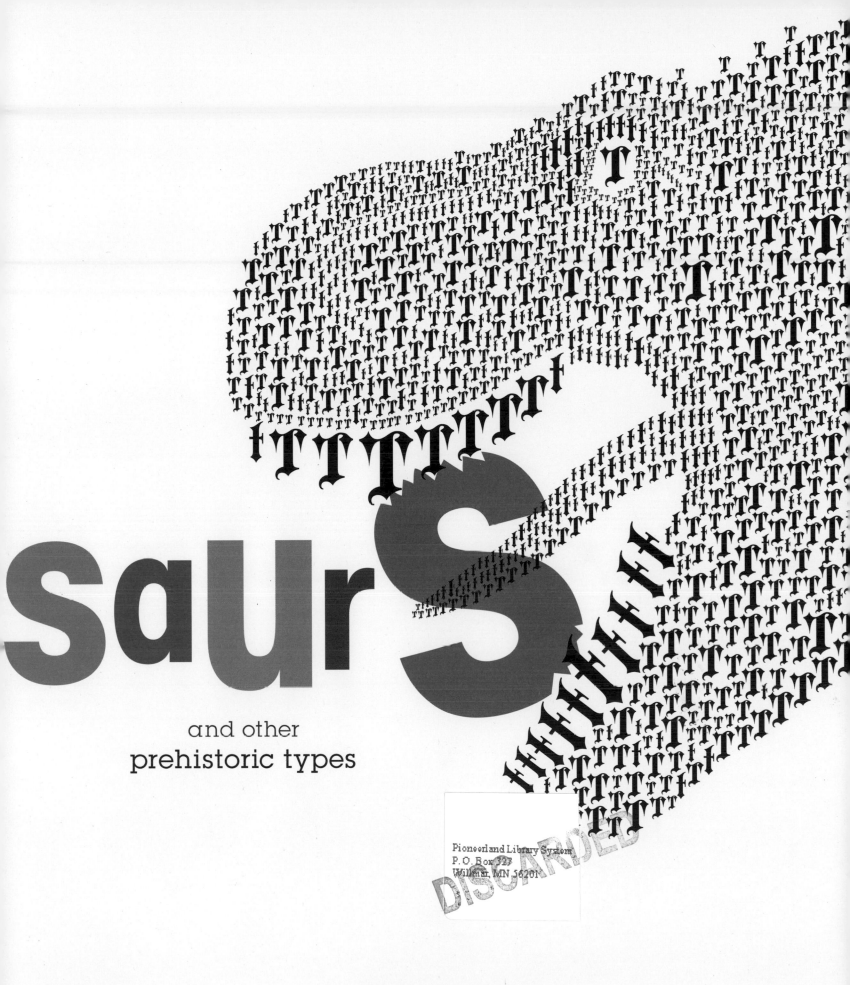

saurs

and other
prehistoric types

by Sharon Werner and Sarah Forss

BLUE  APPLE

SCARY and scaly,
LUMBERING and lumpy,
FAST and ferocious,
big, broad and bumpy.

From up north to down south,
from west to east,

The earth was once home to magnificent beasts.

Now most of you reading this probably know

That dinosaurs lived a long time ago.

Not hundreds or thousands of years in the past.

It's been hundreds of millions

since they were here last.

Dinosaurs lived during **3** different times,

More correctly called **periods**

(which is too hard to rhyme).

The earliest period was called the **Triassic**.

250-200 million years ago

The next (and most famous) is known as **Jurassic**.

145-65 million years ago

CRETACEOUS closed with a crash, so some think.

200-145 million years ago

When this period ended, most beasts were **EXTINCT!**

For mere **hundreds** of years, we've been digging up traces

Of dinosaur parts in all sorts of places.

Studying **FOSSILS** from long ago history,

Trying to solve the dinosaur mystery.

Were they all **big**? Were they all **slow**?

Were they all fearsome? The answer is **NO**.

Related to **lizards**? Or more like a **BIRD**?

yes! to both questions (in one simple word).

But not all of these animals were dinosaur creatures

(Though many non-dinos had dino-like features).

Quetzalcoatlus & Rhamphorhynchus were flying reptiles

The definition of **dinosaur** isn't quite fixed.

In this book of beasties, there's a bit of a mix.

So dig into **alphasaurs**, from **A** to **Z**,

Each one created with **typography***

* Typography refers to the way letters look
and how they are used. In our case, they
were used to make dinosaurs!

At 17 feet tall and 4,000 pounds,
"Big Al" was as tall as an **apple** tree and
weighed as much as an **automobile**.

Allosaurus

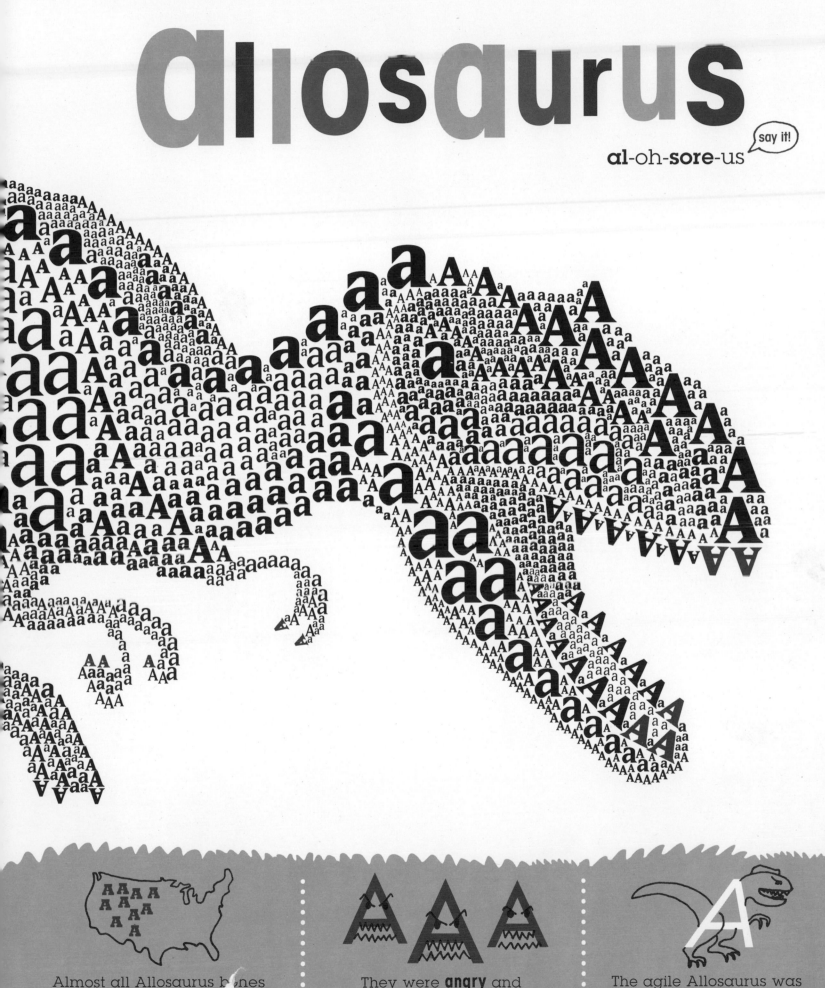

Almost all Allosaurus bones have been found in **America**.

They were **angry** and **aggressive** dinosaurs.

The agile Allosaurus was able to **attack** quickly.

brachiosaurus

brake-ee-oh-**sore**-us

 say it!

The bushy tree tops were an all-day **buffet** for Brachiosaurus, devouring 150 pounds of food just for **breakfast**! That's like you binging on 247 **bagels**, 196 **bananas**, and 333 **bowls** of cereal before school.

This big beast was as tall
as a 4-story **building**.

The quadrupedal (not **bipedal**) Brachiosaurus
walked on four legs. Similar to a giraffe,
its **back** legs were much shorter.

Compsognathus

komp-**sog**-nuh-thus (say it!)

Compsognathus had pincer-like claws on each hand.

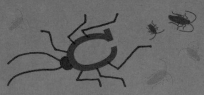

The cute Compsognathus was slightly bigger than a **chicken**.

This carnivore craved **cockroaches** and lizards.

Compsognathus could cruise quickly, like a **cheetah**.

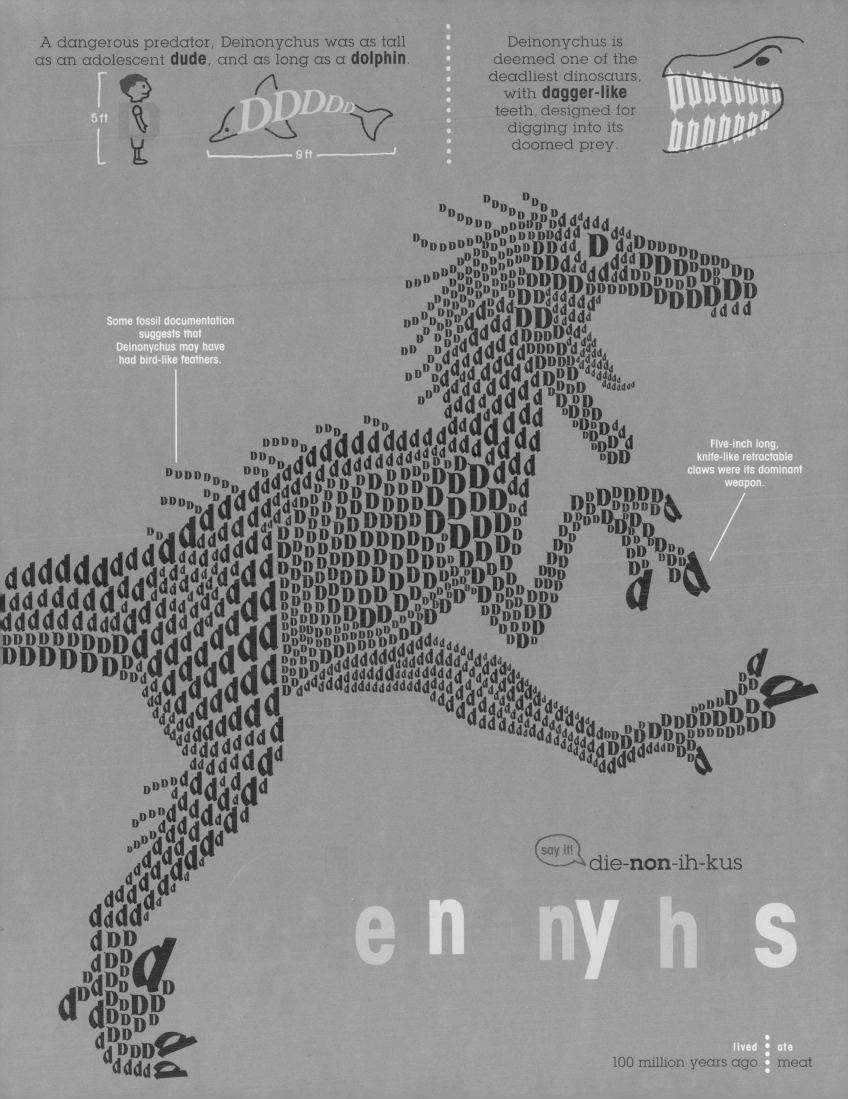

A dangerous predator, Deinonychus was as tall as an adolescent **dude**, and as long as a **dolphin**.

5 ft

9 ft

Deinonychus is deemed one of the deadliest dinosaurs, with **dagger-like** teeth, designed for digging into its doomed prey.

Some fossil documentation suggests that Deinonychus may have had bird-like feathers.

Five-inch long, knife-like retractable claws were its dominant weapon.

say it! die-**non**-ih-kus

e n ny h s

lived : ate
100 million years ago : meat

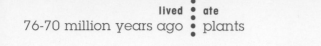

Somewhat similar to a tortoise or armadillo, Euoplocephalus had an extremely hard external shell, and could only be harmed if its unarmored underbelly became exposed.

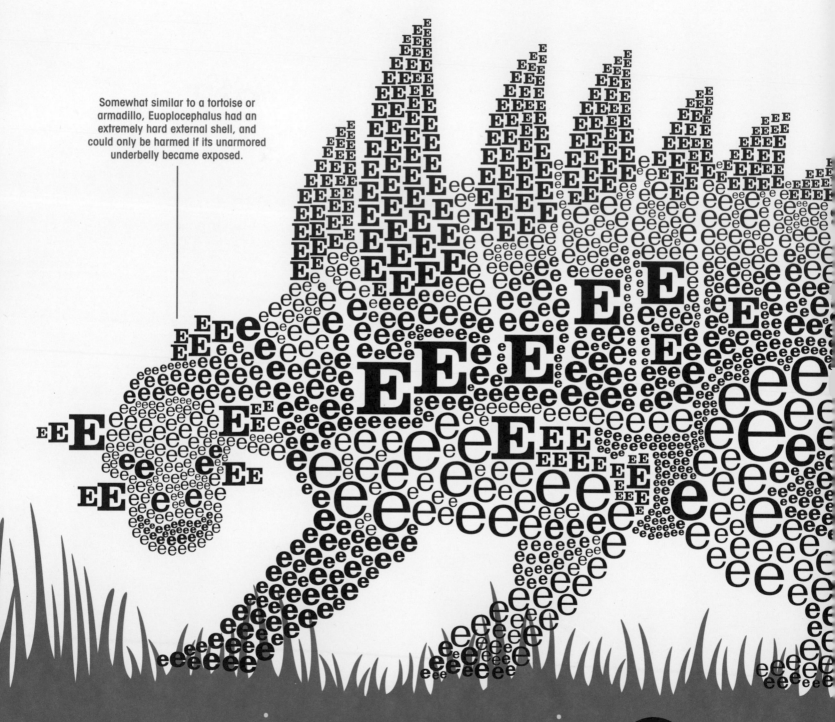

Euoplocephalus was the size of a wee **elephant**.

Its body was entirely armored, even its elbows and **eyelids**.

The elder Euoplocephalus liked to **eat** alone.

euoplocephalus

you-oh-plo-**sef**-ah-lus

say it!

Euoplocephalus's clubbed tail was an effective defense against **enemies**.

T-Rex attacks likely expedited the **extinction** of Euoplocephalus.

40 fossils of the Euoplocephalus have been **excavated** in Montana and Alberta, Canada.

ruitadens

froo-ta-denz

say it!

AT ONLY 26 INCHES LONG FROM ITS FATAL JAWS TO THE TIP OF ITS LONG TAIL, —

Fruitadens were **forest** dwellers feasting on any food they could find and forage.

They were ferocious herd hunters with big **front teeth** to fetch prey and fend off predators.

Fruitadens, the length of a large **ferret**, is the smallest dinosaur found so far.

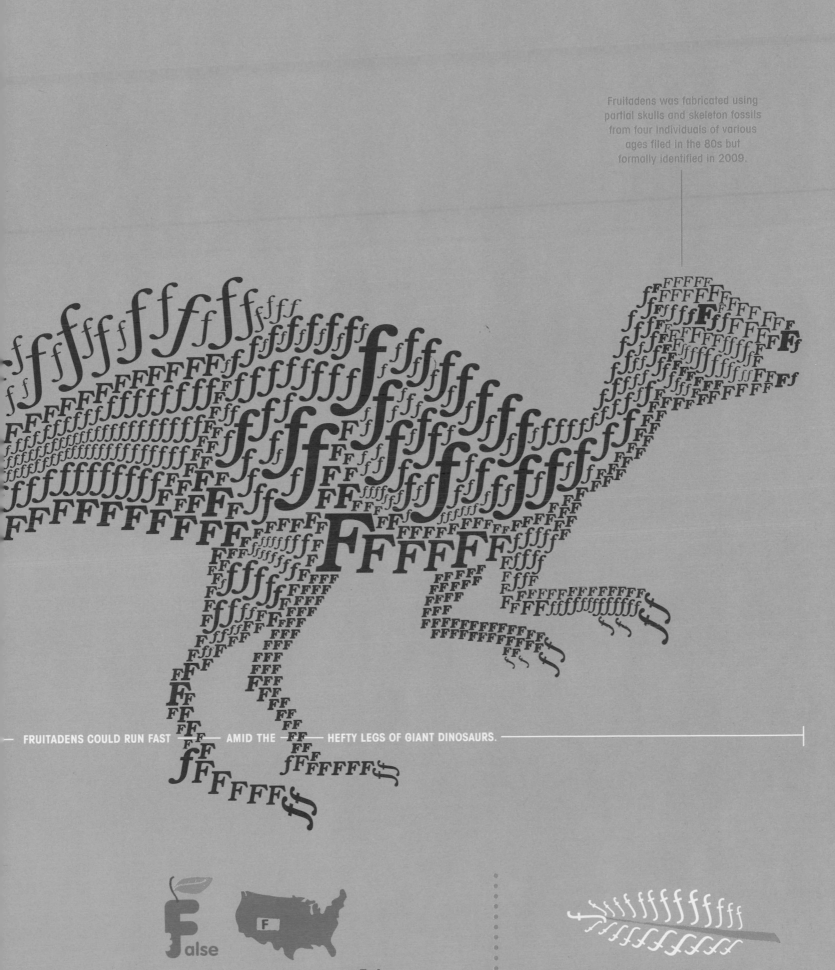

Fruitadens was fabricated using partial skulls and skeleton fossils from four individuals of various ages filed in the 80s but formally identified in 2009.

FRUITADENS COULD RUN FAST — AMID THE — FF — HEFTY LEGS OF GIANT DINOSAURS.

False

True or false: a Fruitadens fed on fruit? **False**. It got that name because it was found in Fruita, Colorado.

Fossils show that Fruitadens may have been festooned with **feathers**.

This guy's great big teeth could grow up to eight inches long. Goodness gracious!

Giganotosaurus was the heaviest carnivore ever to grace the earth, weighing as much as 40 **gorillas**.

Inside that giant noggin was a brain smaller than a **grapefruit**.

Scientists think Giganotosaurus gathered in **groups** to hunt.

giganotosaurus

jy-gah-**noh**-toe-**sore**-us

(say it!)

A **garage** mechanic discovered the first Giganotosaurus fossil in Argentina in 1993.

hydrothero-saurus

say it!

high-droh-**ther**-oh-**sore**-us

Despite its huge body, Hydrotherosaurus's head was hardly 12 inches long.

Its neck had 60 vertebrae and at a whopping 21 feet, it was over half of Hydrotherosaurus's entire body length.

Hydrotherosaurus was as heavy as a **hippopotamus**.

Four flippers helped this hefty reptile high-tail its way through its **H₂O habitat**.

When hungry, he happily **hunted** the sea floor with the help of sand-sifting teeth.

Honestly, this handsome marine reptile is not really a dinosaur at all.

ig-**wahn**-oh-don (say it!)

iguanodon

Impressive 2- to 6-inch spiked thumbs were utilized to impale predators.

I.D.
NAME: Iguana-Tooth
AGE: old

Important: Iguanodon was one of the initial dinosaurs to be **identified**.

Incidentally, Iguanodons were immense, weighing as much as 777 pet **iguanas**.

An **immature** Iguanodon walked upright; as it aged it idled along on four legs.

jinfeng-opteryx

say it!

jin-feng-**op**-ter-ix

Jinfengopteryx is judged to have been the size of a jaunty **jackrabbit**.

Jinfengopteryx had an enlarged **javelin-like** claw.

This Jurassic jetsetter had a **jacket** of feathers but didn't fly around.

Not highly knowledgeable, Kentrosaurus had a **kiwi**-sized brain but a keen sense of smell.

Its double row of spikes were as sharp as **knight's knives**.

Knobby plates on Kentrosaurus's back may have been **key** in keeping it a comfortable temperature.

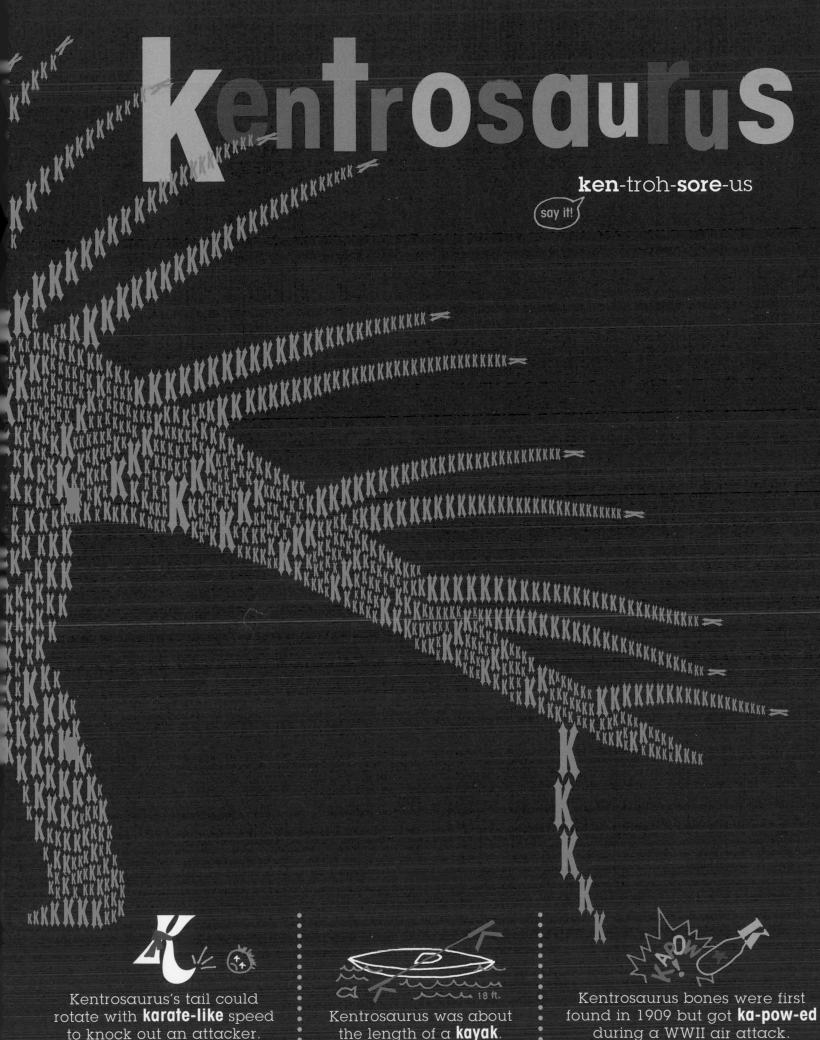

Kentrosaurus

ken-troh-**sore**-us

say it!

Kentrosaurus's tail could rotate with **karate-like** speed to knock out an attacker.

Kentrosaurus was about the length of a **kayak**.

18 ft.

Kentrosaurus bones were first found in 1909 but got **ka-pow-ed** during a WWII air attack.

say it!

lam-bee-oh-**sore**-us

Lambeosaurus

Strong, lean tendons made it possible for Lambeosaurus to keep its large tail level, lending it good balance.

Lambeosaurus is **labeled** as the **largest** duck-billed dinosaur.

This four-legged lizard lacked defenses or armor to look after itself, but at least it ran **lickety**-split.

Lambeosaurus lived in low-lying areas like **lagoons**, lakes, and flood plains.

This hollow lump grew to full size late in life.

Lambeosaurus is named after its locater, Lawrence Lambe, not after a little **lamb**.

Lambeosaurus had lots of **leaf**-shaped teeth.

A large, hollow lump on its head was blown loudly, like a horn, allowing **lads** to locate a **lass**.

microRaptor

my-croh-**rap**-tore

say it!

Microraptor had more wings than modern day birds and many long contour feathers.

Microraptor was a mini dinosaur, about the size of a **muskrat**.

Gliding using all four wings was Microraptor's means of **motion**.

N W · E S

BIRD   DINOSAUR

Microraptors provide a **map** to the mysterious link between birds and dinosaurs.

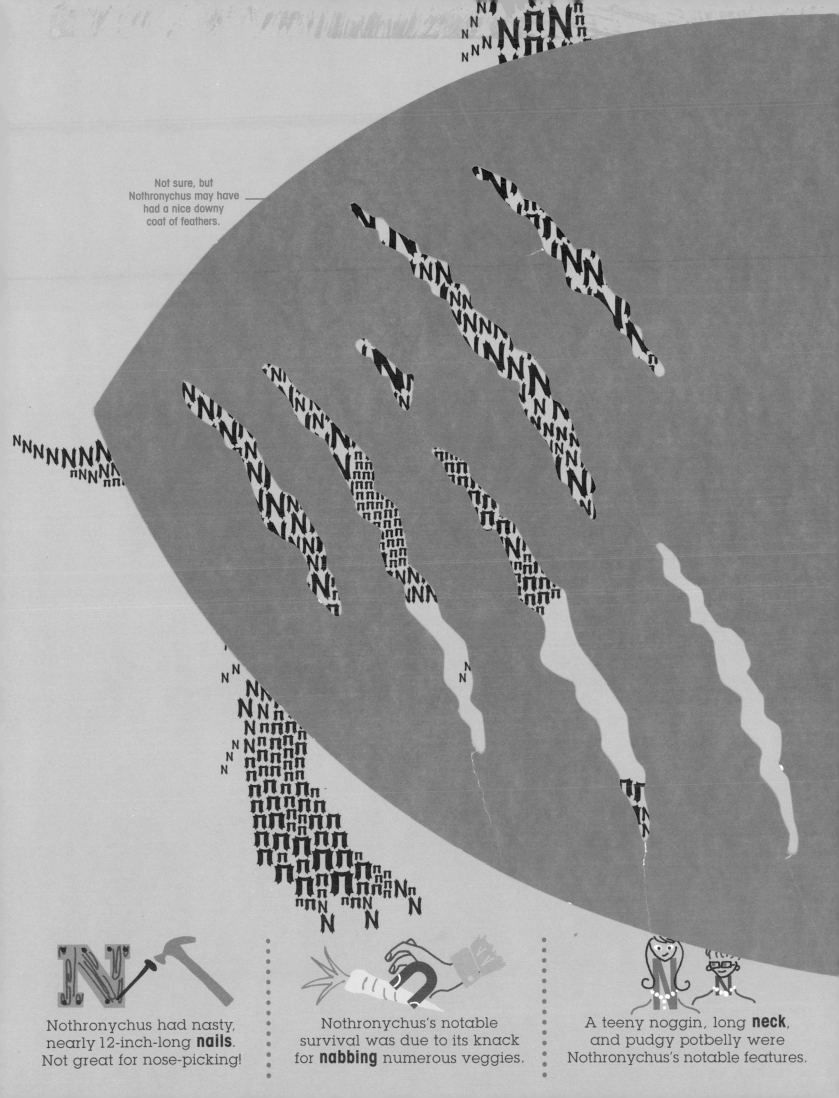

Not sure, but Nothronychus may have had a nice downy coat of feathers.

Nothronychus had nasty, nearly 12-inch-long **nails**. Not great for nose-picking!

Nothronychus's notable survival was due to its knack for **nabbing** numerous veggies.

A teeny noggin, long **neck**, and pudgy potbelly were Nothronychus's notable features.

OuranOsauRuS

oo-**rahn**-oh-**sore**-us

say it!

Scientists have opposing opinions on the objective of the large, sail-like fin; one possible function was to keep Ouranosaurus from overheating, another was to attract mates, or it may have helped make it appear ominous to predators.

Ouranosaurus weighed over four tons, about the size of an **Orca** occupying the ocean.

It gobbled leaves, **oats** and other organic vegetation.

Ouranosaurus's duck-billed skull was **oblong**.

Ouranosaurus was found in the Sahara of Africa when this now arid desert region was filled with marshes and swamps.

Observe the odd sail-like fin, which cooled Ouranosaurus and kept it from overheating.

parasaurolop

par-ah-saw-**rah**-luh-fus

(say it!)

Paleontologists think
Parasaurolophus used its **powerful**
tail as protection from predators.

This paticular prehistoric dino was
as long as 50 **pencils** placed tip to tip.

hus

A peculiar hollow tube was perched on Parasaurolophus's head like a **party** horn.

The purpose of the tube is perplexing. Perhaps it was for the pursuit of a **partner**.

Parasaurolophus preferred to peck **pine** needles and plant parts from high places.

say it! **ket**-zal-coh-**at**-lus

Quetzalcoatlus

Five queen-size **quilts** aren't quite as big as Quetzalcoatlus's 36-foot wingspan.

Quetzalcoatlus were named for the Aztec god, **Quetzalcoatl**.

Quick **question**: did they have feathers? No one knows.

Rhamphorhynchus may have had a pelican-like throat pouch.

say it!

ram-foh-**ring**-kus

rhamphorhynchus

With a wingspan the length of a **reindeer**, Rhamphorhynchus was relatively small.

Rhamphorhynchus had a really long tail with a diamond-shaped **rudder**.

Rhamphorhynchus flew well, but its tiny legs made it a rotten **runner**.

say it!

spine-oh-**sore**-us

Spinosaurus

Spinosaurus's spine sported a **sail-like** structure.

This strapping beast had a six-foot skull and a **snout** like a crocodile.

Spinosaurus was a scavenger who scarfed down **seafood** and scurrying animals.

Spinosaurus got its name from its six-foot high spiny tail.

It had a special **smile** with strikingly straight teeth.

Scientists suspect that Spinosaurus was super **smart**.

It was the largest known carnivore. If it sat on a **softball** field it could stretch from first to second base.

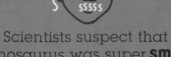

triceratops

say it! try-**sair**-uh-tops

Triceratops had a **toothless**, parrot-like beak.

This **tank-sized** three-horned dino wasn't teeny tiny!

The "frill" could be up to seven feet wide.

There are two theories to explain the Triceratops frill: to terrify attackers or to **tempt** mates.

The thick-skinned Triceratops sometimes traveled in **troops**.

When the Triceratops was in trouble, it could **target** its antagonist with its trio of horns, two of which were an intimidating three feet long.

Utahraptor was **unrivaled** 1,500 lbs. It was unafraid much larger than itself.

Watch out!
The "thagomizer" tail with its four spikes
was good for whacking away attackers.

Its wide hips made it **wiggle**
and waddle when it walked.

Its spiky tail was
a wicked **weapon**.

Two rows of bony plates winding down
its back may have worked to cool
the dino when it was too **warm**.

Xenoposeidon

zen-**oh**-poh-**sye**-don say it!

The only known existing Xenoposeidon bone was excavated in East **Susse**x, England, in 1890.

This single bone was **bo**x**ed** and indexed incorrectly for 113 years, until it was re-examined and the mix-up was fixed.

"Raptor" means "thief."
They were the vandals of
the prehistoric world.

Velociraptor

veh-**los**-ih-**rap**-tore

say it!

A Velociraptor was about as
tall as a **vulture** and as long
as a vacuum cleaner hose.

It used its retractable claws to
violently attack **vulnerable** prey.

These vicious **villains**
were very intelligent.

WuerhoSauruS

woo-**ehr**-hoh-**sore**-us

say it!

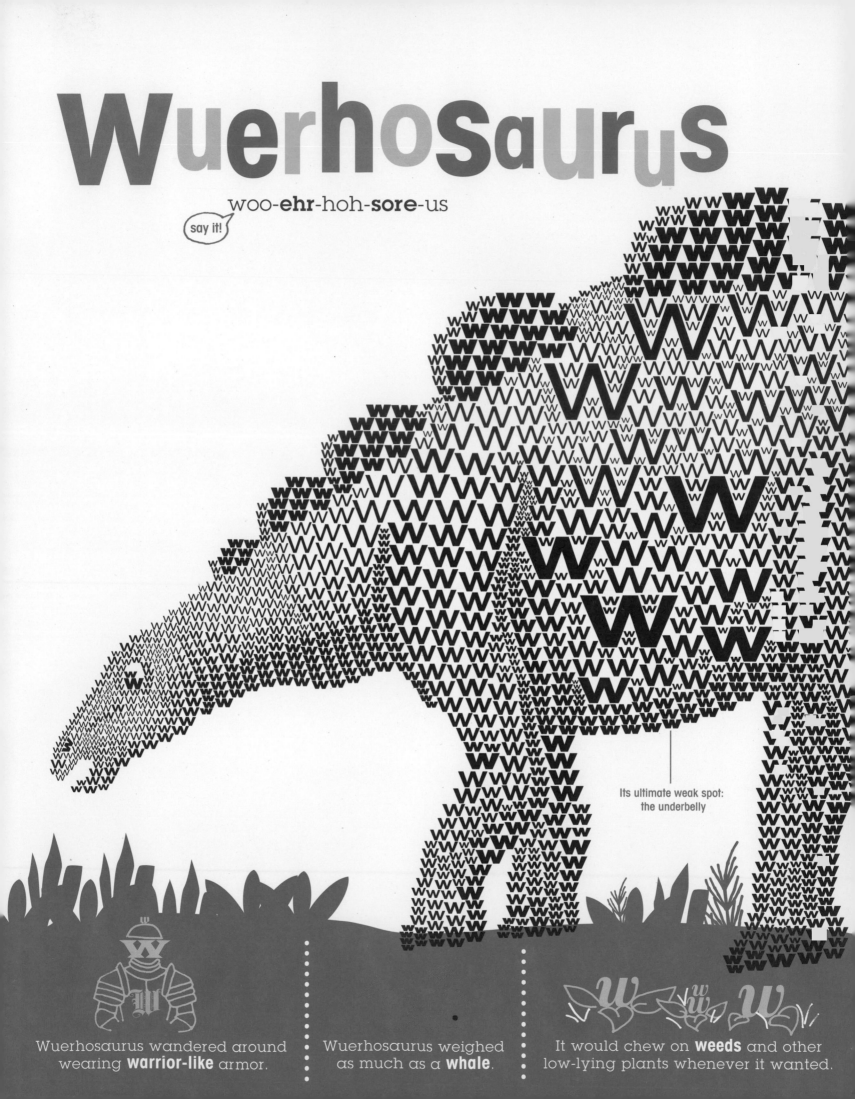

Its ultimate weak spot:
the underbelly

Wuerhosaurus wandered around
wearing **warrior-like** armor.

Wuerhosaurus weighed
as much as a **whale**.

It would chew on **weeds** and other
low-lying plants whenever it wanted.

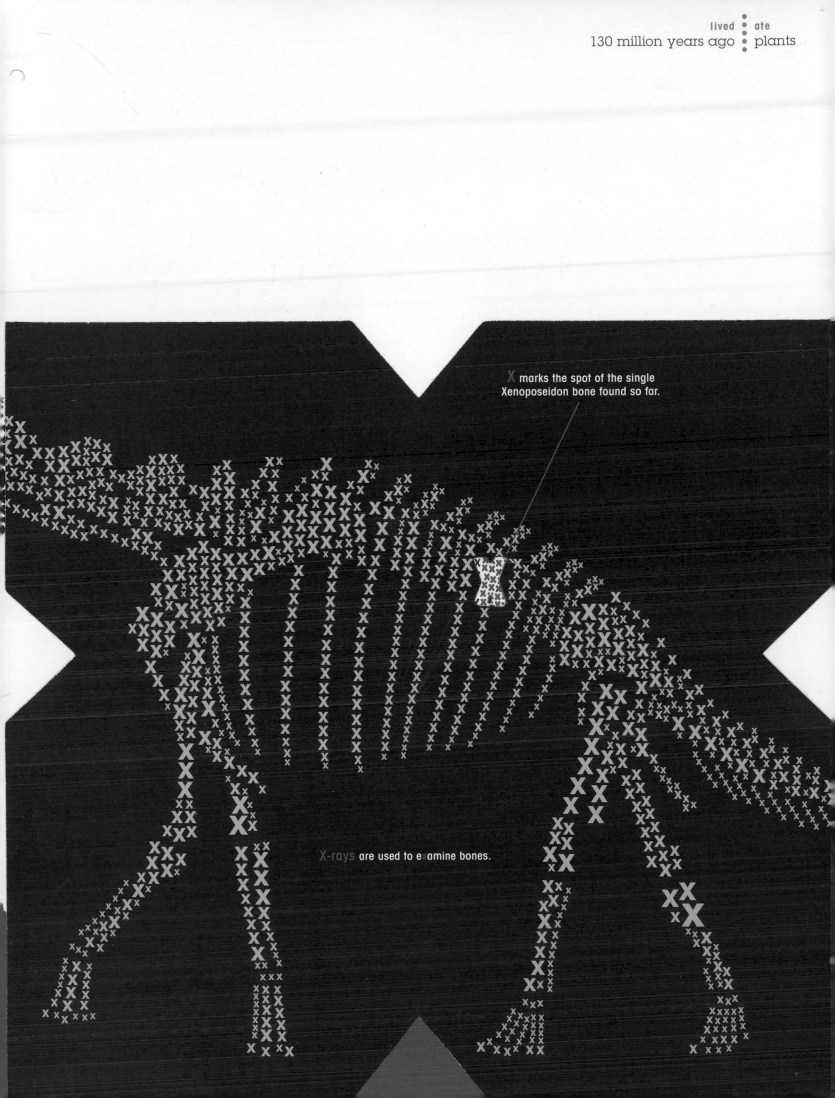

X marks the spot of the single
Xenoposeidon bone found so far.

X-rays are used to examine bones.

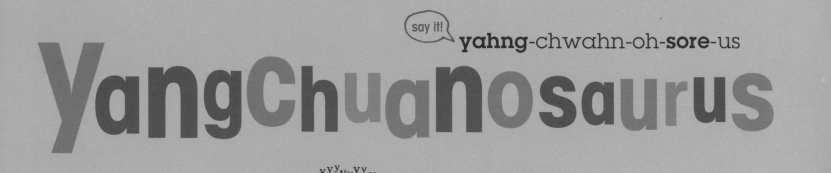

YangChuanosaurus

Yangchuanosaurus had a huge **yawn**—its skull was one yard long.

Was the Yangchuanosaurus as big as a **yacht**? Yep!

It was a fierce predator who didn't **yield** to other dinosaurs.

Yangchuanosaurus was found in the
year 1977 in China's **Yellow River** valley.

Zuniceratops

zoo-nee-**sair**-uh-tops

(say it!)

An 8-year-old boy with a **zest** for dino hunting discovered the Zuniceratops.

The "frill"–that gizmo on its head–puzzles zoologists. Most agree that it wasn't used for zapping **zombies**.

The "eyebrow horns" were as big as prize **zucchinis**.

Zuniceratops means "Zuni-horned head." The **Zuni** are North American Indians.

PLEASE DO NOT FEED THE LIZARD

KOMODO DRAGON

3 ft

10 ft

Zuniceratops was about the size of a Komodo Dragon that you might see zipping around at the **ZOO**.

Here are some interesting things we learned:

Everything that is known about dinosaurs was learned from fossils. **FOSSILS** are any part—or trace—of an animal that lived a long time ago. When fossils are dug up or found, they are examined by scientists called **paleontologists**.

Dinosaur bones aren't actually **BONES**, but instead the minerals left behind and transformed from what was once a bone. These **mineral deposits** keep the shape of the bone, even on the inside, so most people still call them bones.

Dinosaur fossils have been found on every continent on Earth.

Yes, even Antarctica!

Paleontologists look at the rock or dirt that surrounds the fossil to calculate how old it is. Scientists have identified several periods of time when different kinds of dinosaurs lived. At the end of each period there was a **BIG** change on Earth, and most living things became extinct.* These periods are called **TRIASSIC**, **Jurassic**, and **CRETACEOUS**, and all together they make up what's known as the Mesozoic Era (sometimes called "the Time of the Dinosaurs").

No one knows for sure what caused the dinosaurs to vanish, but there are many theories. Were they wiped out by a giant meteor? A volcanic eruption? Did it get too hot? Too cold?

What do you think?

* Extinct means they all died...every last one.

The Alphasaurs in this book were created letter by letter, one dinosaur at a time. We imagined ourselves paleontologists, carefully reconstructing the skeleton of each dinosaur bone by bone. It's exciting and tediously careful work. Creating these creatures of type is a little like digital needlepoint.

If you look closely, you'll notice there is a unique typeface for each Alphasaur. We selected the letter style that we imagined would match the personality or characteristics of each dinosaur.

We love typefaces and thought you might like to know the ones that we used to make our Alphasaurs come to life on these pages.

A • **Allosaurus:** Filosophia

B • **Brachiosaurus:** Universe Condensed

C • **Compsognathus:** Kabel

D • **Deinonychus:** Deutsch Gothic

E • **Euoplocephalus:** Clarendon

F • **Fruitadens:** Bookman Italic

G • **Giganotosaurus:** Elephant

H • **Hydrotherosaurus:** Radio

I • **Iguanodon:** Optima

J • **Jinfengopteryx:** Eames

K • **Kentrosaurus:** Ironwood

L • **Lambeosaurus:** American Typewriter

M • **Microraptor:** Avenir

N • **Nothronychus:** Luciferius

O • **Ouranosaurus:** House Gothic

P • **Parasaurolophus:** Chalet

Q • **Quetzalcoatlus:** New Century Schoolbook Italic

R • **Rhamphorhynchus:** Bauhaus

S • **Spinosaurus:** FutstencilSerif

T • **Triceratops/T-Rex:** Memphis/Blackletter

U • **Utahraptor:** Esprit

V • **Velociraptor:** Mason

W • **Wuerhosaurus:** Bureau Gothic Wide

X • **Xenoposeidon:** Helvetica Rounded & Regular

Y • **Yangchuanosaurus:** Cheltenham

Z • **Zuniceratops:** Hoefler Text Italic

TRIASSIC PERIOD • TRIASSIC PERIOD • TRIASSIC PERIOD • TRIASSIC PERIOD • TRIASSIC PERIOD • TRIASSIC PERIOD • TRIASSIC PERIOD • TRIASSIC PERIOD • TRIASSIC PERIOD • TRIASS

AGROSAURUS ALWALKERIA ANTETONITRUS ARIZONASAURUS ASYLOSAURUS

CASEOSAURUS CHINDESAURUS COELOPHYSIS COLORADISAURUS CRYPTORAPTOR D

CRETACEOUS PERIOD • CRETACEOUS PERIOD • CRETACEOUS PERIOD • CRETACEOUS PERIOD • CRETACEOUS PERIOD • CRETACEOUS PERIOD • CRETACEOUS

ABELISAURUS ACHELOUSAURUS ACHILLOBATOR ACROCANTHOSAURUS AEGYPTOSAURUS AFROVENATOR ALAMOSAURUS ALBERTACERATOPS ALBERTOSAURUS
ANTARCTOSAURUS ARAGOSAURUS ARALOSAURUS ARCHAEOCERATOPS ARGENTINOSAURUS ARRHINOCERATOPS ATLASCOPCOSAURUS
BRACHYLOPHOSAURUS BUITRERAPTOR CARCHARODONTOSAURUS CARNOTAURUS CAUDIPTERYX CHIRAPELTA CENTROSAURUS CHASMOSAURUS CHUBUTIS

CRETACEOUS PERIOD • CRETACEOUS PERIOD • CRETACEOUS PERIOD • CRETACEOUS PERIOD • CRETACEOUS PERIOD • CRETACEOUS PERIOD • CRETACE

JURASSIC PERIOD • JURASSIC PERIOD • JURASSIC PERIOD • JURASSIC PERIOD • JURASSIC PERIOD • JURASSIC PERIOD • JURASSIC PERIOD • JURASSIC PERIOD

JURASSIC PERIOD, 200-145 MILLION YEARS AGO • KNOWN AS THE AGE OF REPTILES • AT THE BEGI

JURASSIC PERIOD • JURASSIC PERIOD • JURASSIC PERIOD • JURASSIC PERIOD • JURASSIC PERIOD • JURASSIC PERIOD • JURASSIC PERIOD • JURASSIC PE

AARDONYX AGILISAURUS ALLOSAURUS AMMOSAURUS AMYGDALODON ANCHISAURUS APATOSAURUS ARCHAEOPTERYX BARAPASAURUS BAROSAURUS BELLUSAU
CHINSHAKIANGOSAURUS CHIROSTENOTES CHUNGKINGOSAURUS COELURUS COMPSOGNATHUS CRYOLOPHOSAURUS DACENTRURUS DATOUSAUR

JURASSIC PERIOD • JURASSIC PERIOD • JURASSIC PERIOD • JURASSIC PERIOD • JURASSIC PERIOD • JURASSIC PERIOD • JURASSIC PERIOD • JURASSIC PERIO

CRETACEOUS PERIOD • CRETACEOUS PERIOD • CRETACEOUS PERIOD • CRETACEOUS PERIOD • CRETACEOUS PERIOD • CRETACEOUS PERIOD • CRETACEOUS

DRAVIDOSAURUS DROMAEOSAURUS DROMICEIOMIMUS DRYPTOSAURUS EDMONTONIA EDMONTOSAURUS EINIOSAURUS EOLAMBIA EOTYRA

CRETACEOUS PERIOD, 145-65 MILLION YEARS AGO • THE EARTH'S CLIMATE WAS COOLING, BUT IT WAS STILL RELATIV
FREQUENT VOLCANIC ACTIVITY • AS THE EARTH SHIFTED, THE CONTINENTS MOVED AND TOOK ON THEIR MODERN-

GIGANOTOSAURUS GILMOREOSAURUS GOBISAURUS GORGOSAURUS GOYOCEPHALE GRACILICERATOPS GRYPOSAURUS HADROSAURUS HA

CRETACEOUS PERIOD • CRETACEOUS PERIOD • CRETACEOUS PERIOD • CRETACEOUS PERIOD • CRETACEOUS PERIOD • CRETACEOUS PERIOD • CRE

TRIASSIC PERIOD • TRIASSIC PERIOD • TRIASSIC PERIOD • TRIASSIC PERIOD • TRIASSIC PERIOD • TRIASSIC PERIOD • TRIASSIC PERIOD • TRIASSIC PERIOD • TR

FABROSAURUS GOJIRASAURUS GUAIBASAURUS HALTICOSAURUS HERREF

TRIASSIC PERIOD • TRIASSIC PERIOD • TRIASSIC PERIOD • TRIASSIC PERIOD • TRIASSIC PERIOD • TRIASSIC PERIOD • TRIASSIC PERIOD • TRIASSIC P

JURASSIC PERIOD • JURASSIC PERIOD • JURASSIC PERIOD • JURASSIC PERIOD • JURASSIC PERIOD • JURASSIC PERIOD • JURASSIC PERIOD • JURAS

EUSTREPTOSPONDYLUS GARGOYLEOSAURUS GASOSAURUS GIRAFFATITAN GUANLONG HAPLOCANTHOSAUR
KENTROSAURUS KOTASAURUS LAPPARENTOSAURUS LESOTHOSAURUS LEXOVISAURUS LOPHOSTROPHEUS L

JURASSIC PERIOD • WITH THE SPLIT OF THE PANGAEA THERE WAS MORE WATER SURROUNDING THE TWO LANDMASSES. THIS C

JURASSIC PERIOD • JURASSIC PERIOD • JURASSIC PERIOD • JURASSIC PERIOD • JURASSIC PERIOD • JURASSIC PERIOD • JURASSIC PERIOD • JURASSIC PERIOD • JU

TRIASSIC PERIOD • TRIASSIC PERIOD • TRIASSIC PERIOD • TRIASSIC PERIOD • TRIASSIC PERIOD • TRIASSIC PERIOD • TRIASSIC PERIOD • TRIASSIC PER

TRIASSIC PERIOD, 250-200 MILLION YEARS AGO • THIS IS A TIME OF RECOVERY FOR THE EARTH

TRIASSIC PERIOD • TRIASSIC PERIOD • TRIASSIC PERIOD • TRIASSIC PERIOD • TRIASSIC PERIOD • TRIASSIC PERIOD • TRIASSIC PERIOD • TRIASSIC PER

LILIENSTERNUS LOPHOSTROPHEUS LYCORHINUS LYSTROSAURUS MASTODONS

TRIASSIC PERIOD • TRIASSIC PERIOD • TRIASSIC PERIOD • TRIASSIC PERIOD • TRIASSIC PERIOD • TRIASSIC PERIOD • TRIASSIC PERIOD • TRIASSI

CRETACEOUS PERIOD • CRETACEOUS PERIOD • CRETACEOUS PERIOD • CRETACEOUS PERIOD • CRETACEOUS PERIOD • CRETACEOUS PERIOD • CRETACEOUS PERIOD

CRETACEOUS PERIOD • THERE'S EVIDENCE THERE MAY HAVE BEEN SNOWFALL ON THE TOPS OF THE HIGHER MOUN
ACTIVITY DURING THE LATE CRETACEOUS, THE EARTH ONCE AGAIN WARMED UP • THE CRETACEOUS SAW A DIVE

CRETACEOUS PERIOD • CRETACEOUS PERIOD • CRETACEOUS PERIOD • CRETACEOUS PERIOD • CRETACEOUS PERIOD • CRETACEOUS PERIOD • CRETACEO

ISISAURUS JAXARTOSAURUS JINZHOUSAURUS JOBARIA KHAAN KRITOSAURUS LAMACERATOPS LAMBEOSAURUS LEAELLYNASAURA LEO
MALAWISAURUS MAPUSAURUS MASIAKASAURUS MAXAKALISAURUS MICROCERATOPS MICROPACHYCEPHALOSAURUS MICRORAPTOR MINMI MUTTABURRASAU
OPISTHOCOELICAUDIA ORNITHOMIMUS ORODROMEUS ORYCTODROMEUS OURANOSAURUS OVIRAPTOR PACHYCEPHALOSAURUS PACHYRHINOSAURUS PARO

CRETACEOUS PERIOD • CRETACEOUS PERIOD • CRETACEOUS PERIOD • CRETACEOUS PERIOD • CRETACEOUS PERIOD • CRETACEOUS PERIOD • CRETACEOUS PERIOD • C

JURASSIC PERIOD • JUNGLES AND FLOWERING PLANTS WERE BEGINNING TO CHANGE THE FACE OF THE EARTH • DINOSA

JURASSIC PERIOD • JURASSIC PERIOD • JURASSIC PERIOD • JURASSIC PERIOD • JURASSIC PERIOD • JURASSIC PERIOD • JURASSIC PERIOD • JURASSIC PERIOD

MONOLOPHOSAURUS NQWEBASAURUS OMEISAURUS ORNITHOLESTES OTHNIELIA PATAGOSAURUS PIATNITZKYSAURUS PODOKES

JURASSIC PERIOD • JURASSIC PERIOD • JURASSIC PERIOD • JURASSIC PERIOD • JURASSIC PERIOD • JURASSIC PERIOD • JURASSIC PERIOD • JURASSIC PERIOD • JURASSIC PE

TRIASSIC PERIOD • TRIASSIC PERIOD • TRIASSIC PERIOD • TRIASSIC PERIOD • TRIASSIC PERIOD • TRIASSIC PERIOD • TRIASSIC PERIOD • TRIASSIC PE

PISANOSAURUS PLATEOSAURUS PROCOMPSOGNATHUS PROGANOCHELYS PROTOA

TRIASSIC PERIOD • DURING THE TRIASSIC, ALMOST ALL THE EARTH'S LAND WAS STUCK TOGETHER IN

TRIASSIC PERIOD • TRIASSIC PERIOD • TRIASSIC PERIOD • TRIASSIC PERIOD • TRIASSIC PERIOD • TRIASSIC PERIOD • TRIASSIC PERIOD • TRIASSIC PERIOD •

CRETACEOUS PERIOD • CRETACEOUS PERIOD • CRETACEOUS PERIOD • CRETACEOUS PERIOD • CRETACEOUS PERIOD • CRETACEOUS PERIOD • CRETACEOUS PERIOD • C

CRETACEOUS PERIOD • DINOSAUR SPECIES BECAME TREMENDOUSLY DIVERSE AND LARGER AS THEY ADAP

POLACANTHUS PRENOCEPHALE PROSAUROLOPHUS PROTARCHAEOPTERYX PROTOCERATOPS PSITTACOSAURUS QUAESITOSAURUS
SHANAG SHANTUNGOSAURUS SHUVUUIA SINOCALLIOPTERYX SINOSAUROPTERYX SINVENATOR SONIDOSAURUS SPINOSAURUS STEGOCERAS STRU

KNOW EXACTLY WHY • AT THE END OF THE CRETACEOUS, MANY PLANTS WERE WIPED OUT, CAUSING THE HER

TENONTOSAURUS THESCELOSAURUS TOROSAURUS TRICERATOPS TROODON TSINTAOSAURUS TYLOCEPHALE TYRANNOSAURUS UDANOCERATO

CRETACEOUS PERIOD • CRETACEOUS PERIOD • CRETACEOUS PERIOD • CRETACEOUS PERIOD • CRETACEOUS PERIOD • CRETACEOUS PERIOD • CRETACEOUS PERIOD

TRIASSIC PERIOD • TRIASSIC PERIOD • TRIASSIC PERIOD • TRIASSIC PERIOD • TRIASSIC PERIOD • TRIASSIC PERIOD • TRIASSIC PERIOD • TRIASSIC PERIOD • TRIASSIC

SELLOSAURUS SPONDYLOSOMA STAURIKOSAURUS SYNTARSUS TAWA TECHNOSAU

TRIASSIC PERIOD • THE EARTH'S CLIMATE WAS HOT AND DRY • AT THE BEGINNING OF THE TRIASSIC, TH

TRIASSIC PERIOD • TRIASSIC PERIOD • TRIASSIC PERIOD • TRIASSIC PERIOD • TRIASSIC PERIOD • TRIASSIC PERIOD • TRIASSIC PERIOD • TRIASSIC PERIOD •

JURASSIC PERIOD • JURASSIC PERIOD • JURASSIC PERIOD • JURASSIC PERIOD • JURASSIC PERIOD • JURASSIC PERIOD • JURASSIC PERIOD • JURASSIC PERIO

SEGISAURUS SEISMOSAURUS SHUNOSAURUS SINRAPTOR STEGOSAURUS TORVOSAURUS TUOJIANGOSAURUS VULCA

JURASSIC PERIOD • MARINE REPTILES SUCH AS ICHTHYOSAURS AND PLESIOSAURS, AND GIANT CROCODILES RUL

JURASSIC PERIOD • JURASSIC PERIOD • JURASSIC PERIOD • JURASSIC PERIOD • JURASSIC PERIOD • JURASSIC PERIOD • JURASSIC PERIOD • JURASSIC PERIOD • JURASSIC PERIOD •